DISCARD

Profiles in Greek and Roman Mythology

HERCULES

Mitchell Lane
PUBLISHERS

P.O. Box 196
Hockessin, Delaware 19707
Visit us on the web: www.mitchelllane.com
Comments? email us: mitchelllane@mitchelllane.com

PROFILES IN GREEK AND ROMAN MYTHOLOGY

Profiles in Greek and Roman Mythology

HERCULES

Jim Whiting

Mitchell Lane
PUBLISHERS

P.O. Box 196
Hockessin, Delaware 19707
Visit us on the web: www.mitchelllane.com
Comments? email us: mitchelllane@mitchelllane.com

Printing   1   2   3   4   5   6   7   8   9

Library of Congress Cataloging-in-Publication Data
Whiting, Jim, 1943–
     Hercules / by Jim Whiting.
        p. cm. — (Profiles in Greek and Roman mythology)
     Includes bibliographical references and index.
     ISBN 978-1-58415-553-9 (library bound)
     1. Heracles (Greek mythology)—Juvenile literature. I. Title.
BL820.H5W45 2007
398.20938'02—dc22
                                                                      2007000772

ABOUT THE AUTHOR: Jim Whiting has been a remarkably versatile and accomplished journalist, writer, editor, and photographer for more than 30 years. He has made seven trips to Greece, during which time he immersed himself in the country's fabulous history and culture. A voracious reader since early childhood, Mr. Whiting has written and edited more than 250 nonfiction children's books on a wide range of topics. He lives in Washington state with his wife and two teenage sons.

PHOTO CREDITS: p. 6—House of the Vettii, Pompeii; p. 12—Jonathan Scott; p. 22—Edward-Burne Jones; p. 28—Victoria and Albert Museum; p. 32—The State Heritage Museum; p. 36—Barbara Marvis.

AUTHOR'S NOTE: In this book, the Roman version of the hero's name, *Hercules*, has been used. It is the one by which most Americans know him. To the Greeks, he was known as Heracles (HAYR-uh-kleez). All the other characters and places in this story are given their Greek names. The legend of Hercules has many variations. This version follows the most commonly told versions. Portions of this story have been retold using dialogue as an aid to readability. The dialogue is based on the author's extensive research and approximates what might have occurred at the time.

     To reflect current usage, we have chosen to use the secular era designations BCE ("before the common era") and CE ("of the common era") instead of the traditional designations BC ("before Christ") and AD (*anno Domini,* "in the year of the Lord").

TABLE OF CONTENTS

Profiles in Greek and Roman Mythology

A wall painting in Pompeii shows the infant Hercules strangling the snakes the goddess Hera sent to kill him. The eruption of Mt. Vesuvius in 79 CE buried the city of Pompeii. Many centuries later its treasures were unearthed.

HERCULES

CHAPTER 1

The Legend Begins

It was a sight that would make anyone run away in fear. A huge lion was returning from a night of hunting. Bloodstains smeared his jaws. Shreds of human flesh clung to his teeth. The lion belched. He had eaten very well that night.

Hercules (HER-kyoo-leez) didn't flinch. Fearlessly, he drew his bow and fired an arrow at the beast. The arrow struck right where he had aimed it, over the beast's heart.

The lion didn't die. In fact, the arrow didn't even stick. It bounced harmlessly away. Hercules didn't realize it yet, but no weapon could pierce the lion's skin. It was as hard as steel or stone. Next Hercules pulled out his sword. It bent harmlessly when he struck the lion. Finally he whacked it on the head with his heavy club. The blow would have crushed the skull of any normal animal, but this animal was different. It was a monster called the Nemean (nuh-MAY-un) Lion.

After being struck with the club, the animal turned away from Hercules. It wasn't injured. The blow had caused some discomfort, a ringing in its ears. It went into its cave to get away from the nuisance.

Hercules knew he had to find a way of killing the Nemean Lion. He strung a net over the entrance to the cave so that the beast couldn't escape. Then he followed the lion deep inside the cave and grabbed it. The lion fought back. It was very strong, but Hercules was even stronger. When the lion started to tire, Hercules put his hands around the lion's throat and began choking it. The animal's struggles became feebler and feebler. Finally it collapsed, dead.

Weapons like knives and spears couldn't penetrate the steel-like skin of the Nemean Lion. Hercules had to kill the beast with his bare hands.

Hercules wasn't finished. He knew that people wouldn't believe he had killed the lion just on his word. He had to cut off its skin, or pelt—firm evidence of what he had done. He drew his knife.

The knife didn't work any better than his arrows or sword had. It wouldn't cut into the lion's extremely tough skin. Hercules grabbed one of the lion's claws and used it instead. It neatly slit open the skin. When he finished, he wrapped the pelt around his body. He knew it would give him extra protection from his enemies. The lion's head rested on top of his own, making him look especially fierce.

Then he went back to the city of Mycenae (my-SEE-nee), where his cousin Eurystheus (yuh-RISS-thee-us) was the ruler. Eurystheus had ordered Hercules to kill the Nemean Lion. He had issued this order believing that the lion would kill Hercules. Eurystheus wanted Hercules dead, because he was afraid that Hercules might try to replace him as the ruler of Mycenae.

Eurystheus was shocked to see Hercules come back alive. Then he relaxed. Hercules was in his power. He had to do whatever Eurystheus asked him to do. Eurystheus knew there were plenty of other monsters and plenty of other difficult tasks. He quickly made plans for another "job" for Hercules, feeling confident that he soon would be rid of his cousin.

The reasons Hercules was in his cousin's power went back many years. It all started with Zeus (ZOOS), the chief Greek god. Zeus often cheated on his wife, Hera (HAYR-uh), and had relationships with mortal women.

Zeus (on the right) was the chief god of the ancient Greeks. He was often unfaithful to his wife, Hera (left). She would become angry and seek revenge.

One of these relationships was with a young woman named Danaë (DAY-nuh-ee). They had a son, whose name was Perseus (PER-see-us). When he grew up, Perseus founded Mycenae and became its first king.[1] He had many children. One of them, Sthenelus (STHEH-nuh-lus), eventually succeeded Perseus as king. Perseus' grandson Amphitryon (am-FIH-tree-on) also wanted to become king. He married a woman named Alcmene (alk-MEE-nee).

One time Amphitryon went off to battle. Zeus took advantage of his absence to disguise himself as Amphitryon and sleep with Alcmene. To Zeus, Alcmene wasn't just any woman. As classical scholars Michael Grant and John Hazel note, she was "the wisest and most beautiful of women."[2] With such a special woman, Zeus knew he would have a special son. To make sure that he was truly extraordinary, Zeus altered time so that three nights seemed like one.

Hera quickly learned about Zeus' relationship with Alcmene. She was very angry and wanted revenge. She made Zeus swear a solemn promise that the next boy born to a descendant of Perseus would become the king of Mycenae. Zeus happily agreed. He was sure that this boy would be Alcmene's son, who would be named Hercules.

Nine months later, Alcmene was about to give birth to Hercules. But Sthenelus' wife was also pregnant. Hera hurried down to earth from Mount Olympus and slowed down Alcmene's birth. As a result, Sthenelus' son Eurystheus was born one hour earlier than Hercules. According to Zeus' promise, Eurystheus was now destined to become the king of Mycenae. Zeus was furious, but there was nothing he could do.

In addition to Hercules, Alcmene also gave birth to another son, Iphicles (IF-ih-kleez), who was Amphitryon's son. Hercules, however, was the one with the power. That became evident several months later. Hera was still seething, so she sent two large poisonous snakes into the room where the two toddlers were sleeping. Iphicles saw the snakes and began crying and screaming. The commotion woke up Hercules. He strangled the snakes, tied them into a knot, and swung the dead serpents over his head.

Even though he was half god, Hercules was brought up in the same way as other mortals. He took lessons just like everyone else. He had the very best tutors in Greece. Some were even descended from the gods.

He studied the lyre with a man named Linus (LY-nus). Linus was said to have descended from Apollo (uh-PAH-loh), the god of music. Because Hercules was much bigger than other boys, his fingers were correspondingly large. It was difficult to do something delicate like plucking the strings of the lyre. Linus often criticized him because he played so poorly. One day Linus was being especially hard on him. Hercules hit him with the lyre, killing him instantly. Hercules was put on trial for the crime, but the jury decided it was a case of self-defense.

As Hercules grew older, he married a woman named Megara (MEH-guh-ruh). They were very happy together, and had three sons.

The Pythia

Hera still wouldn't leave Hercules alone. One day she made him go insane. In a fit of anger, he killed Megara and his sons and threw them into a huge fire.

Then Hera brought back his normal mind. He was heartbroken over the loss of his wife and children. He realized what he had done was wrong, and knew he would have to pay for his crime. He went to the Oracle at Delphi, a famous shrine in Greece. A priestess called the Pythia (PIH-thee-uh) would tell him what he had to do.

The Pythia sat silently for a moment. Then she said, "You must go to your cousin at Mycenae where he is now the king. He will give you twelve tasks. When you have done all of them, you will be free. Your crime will be forgiven."

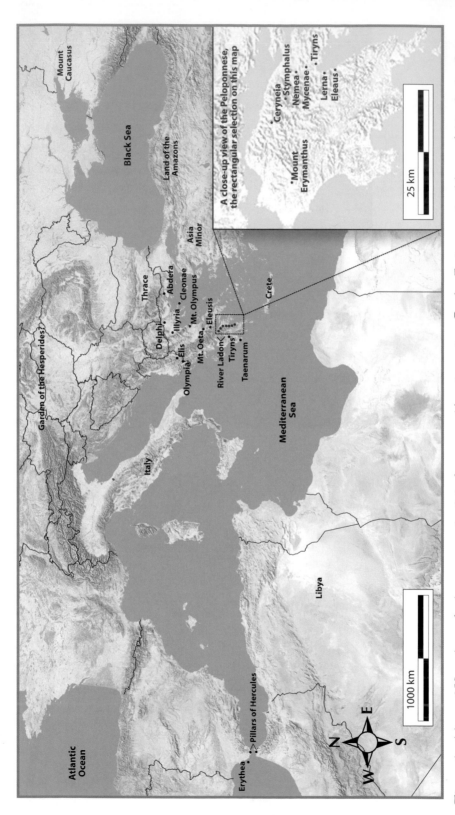

The twelve labors of Hercules took place over much of the known world to the ancient Greeks. Each successive labor took him farther from his home in Mycenae. The last two took him to the Garden of the Hesperides, which may have been far north of Greece, and to Hades, the mythical Underworld.

Zeus' Other Love Affairs

Even though Zeus was the chief god, his character wasn't flawless. He sometimes cheated on his wife. A number of myths describe these love affairs. Here are four of the most famous.

To seduce a beautiful woman named Leda (LEE-duh), Zeus took the form of a swan. There were four children from this union. Two were twin boys: Castor (KAS-tur) and Polydeuces (pah-lih-DOO-seez). They later became the Gemini (JEH-mih-nye), one of the twelve signs of the Zodiac. One of the daughters was Helen. Said to be the most beautiful woman in the world, she was kidnapped by Paris, a prince of Troy. The Greeks waged war against the Trojans to get her back. The other daughter, Clytemnestra (Kly-tem-NES-truh), married Agamemnon (aa-guh-MEM-non), who led the Greeks against Troy.

Zeus also seduced Aegina (ee-GY-nuh). They had a son named Aeacus (EE-uh-kus). Jealous Hera sent a plague to the land that Aeacus ruled. Nearly everyone died. Seeing an anthill, Aeacus prayed that the island be repopulated with as many people as there were ants. Zeus granted his prayer. These new people were called Myrmidons (MEER-mih-dons), after the Greek word for ants. They followed Achilles during the Trojan War.

A third affair was with Semele (SEH-muh-lee). Zeus was so taken with her that he swore to do anything she asked. Hera took revenge on the pregnant woman. She made Semele ask to see Zeus in all his power and glory. He knew that no mortal could withstand that sight, but he had no choice. He had made a promise. Semele was consumed by his lightning. Zeus saved the child and stitched him into his thigh. The child was Dionysus (dy-uh-NY-sus), who became the god of wine.

Europa and the bull

The continent of Europe is named for Europa (yoo-ROH-puh), yet another one of Zeus' conquests. He came to her in the form of a bull and carried her away from her family. They had three sons, Minos (MY-nohs) Rhadamanthys (rad-uh-MAN-this), and Sarpedon (SAR-puh-don).[3] When they were grown, Minos and Rhadamanthys became the judges of people when they arrived in the Underworld.[4]

Hercules had to destroy all the heads of the Lernaean Hydra in order to kill the monster. The problem was that as he destroyed each head, two would immediately replace it. Hercules devised an ingenious scheme to solve the problem.

HERCULES

CHAPTER 2

Labor Days

Eurystheus didn't give Hercules much of a rest after he returned from killing the Nemean Lion. He quickly ordered him to kill the Lernaean (lur-NY-un) Hydra (HY-druh). This monster lived in a swamp. It had a huge body similar to a dog's. It also had nine heads, each one long and snakelike. Its breath caused immediate death. And no one could kill it. If someone cut off one head, two or three would grow back from the gushing blood.[1]

Hercules and his nephew Iolaus (eye-oh-LAY-us) searched for the beast and soon found it. Hercules crushed one of the heads with his club, but two new ones grew back in its place. Meanwhile, Hera sent a large crab to help the Hydra. The crab grabbed Hercules' foot.

Hercules stomped on the crab and smashed it. To reward the crab for trying to help, Hera made it into one of the twelve signs of the Zodiac—the constellation of Cancer.

The crab was gone, but killing it cost Hercules some of his strength. It was getting harder and harder for him to move. The Hydra was gaining the upper hand. Then he had an idea.

"Iolaus," he shouted. "Set that nearby grove of trees on fire. Then light a torch from the flames."

Iolaus did as his uncle requested. Every time Hercules smashed a head, Iolaus cauterized the wound, using the flaming torch to seal the sore. No more blood would flow from the monster, so no new heads could grow.

Gradually Hercules began to overcome the Hydra. Finally only one immortal head was left. Hercules cut it off and buried it under a huge boulder so that it couldn't bother people anymore.

Before he left, he dipped his arrows in the poisonous blood of the beast. Now they were even deadlier than before.

When he reported to Eurystheus, the king claimed that Hercules hadn't really completed the labor. His nephew had helped him.

Hercules answered angrily, "If you don't count it as one of my labors, I'll go back and dig up the head. Then I'll bring it here."

Eurystheus caved. Hercules' second labor would count.

His third labor took him more than a year to complete. He had to capture the Ceryneian (seh-rih-NEE-uhn) Hind. A hind is a kind of deer. This very special deer had golden horns and brass hooves. The goddess Artemis (AR-tuh-mis), who protected all the wild animals of the forest by killing anyone who threatened them, had sworn to protect the hind. Eurystheus chuckled. Surely Hercules would meet his death this time.

After chasing the animal for a year, Hercules caught up with it when it paused to drink at a river. Aiming carefully, he shot an arrow at it. It wasn't one of the poisoned ones, because he didn't want to kill the deer. The arrow pinned the brass hooves together. Hercules could then pick up the hind and carry it over his shoulder.

Suddenly Artemis appeared before him. "I will kill you if you have drawn even a drop of its blood," she said.

"I haven't," Hercules replied. "My arrow only struck its brass hooves."

Hercules knew to treat the gods and goddesses with respect. He humbly told Artemis that he had to show his cousin the deer, and that he would return it when he was finished. She allowed him to take the deer, and Hercules was as good as his word. He brought the golden hind to Artemis after showing the animal to Eurystheus.

Eurystheus was unhappy. Hercules had cheated death three times. Then he thought he had an opportunity. A huge wild boar was terrorizing the people who lived on Mount Erymanthus (er-ih-MAN-thus). Eurystheus ordered Hercules to end the threat presented by the Erymanthian (er-ih-MAN-thee-un) Boar. To make the task even harder, Hercules had to capture it and bring it back alive.

Carrying his club, his bow, and a quiver full of poisoned arrows, Hercules set off. Before he arrived at the mountain, he found a group of centaurs (SEN-tars). These creatures had the body of a horse and the head and torso of a man. He liked them. The chief centaur, Cheiron (KY-ron), had been one of his tutors. Cheiron had instructed Hercules in the art of medicine.

When Hercules arrived, the centaurs were drunk. They started throwing rocks at Hercules. He pulled out his bow and began firing his arrows. Accidentally, one struck Cheiron in the knee. The poison gnawed away at the old centaur, and Hercules sadly watched his former teacher die in agony.

The Ceryneian Hind was so fast that it could even outrun an arrow. Hercules had to be very patient while he was tracking it. He finally captured the animal when it stopped to get a drink of water.

He continued on to the mountain and easily found the boar's trail. The animal had left huge hoofprints in the snow. Hercules saw it hiding in some bushes. It grunted at him threateningly. Quick-

A statue of Hercules capturing the Erymanthian Boar stands in the zoo in Berlin, Germany. After subduing the creature, Hercules had to carry it on his shoulders all the way back to Mycenae.

witted Hercules let out a blood-curdling yell. Startled, the boar turned around and tried to run away. It ran into a snowdrift, lost its balance, and fell over. Hercules jumped on it and tied it up before it could struggle to its feet. Then he carried it back to Eurystheus. Terrified of the Erymanthian Boar, Eurystheus ran and hid in a huge bronze jar.

By the time Eurystheus emerged, Hercules had left the city. He had joined another famous hero, Jason. They were looking for the golden fleece.[2]

When Hercules returned to Mycenae, Eurystheus thought he'd try something different. Hercules had cheated death four times. His next task would be safer but just as hard to complete—or so Eurystheus thought.

Augeas (aw-JEE-us), the king of Elis, owned many cattle and sheep and more than 500 bulls. He kept the beasts in huge stables, which he never cleaned. The manure had piled at least two feet deep. It really stank. Hercules' task was to clean them out in one day.

Augeas laughed. "There is way too much for one person to clean in a year, let alone a single day," he said. "Even if you could, it would be a very filthy, smelly job."

But Hercules was a creative thinker. He dammed up two rivers and diverted them through Augeas' stables. The force of the current swept away all the animal excrement. Soon the stables sparkled like new.

Task number six was getting rid of the birds that infested the Stymphalian (stim-FAY-lee-un) Marsh. They were large birds, about the size of a wading bird called a crane. Their beaks, claws, and feathers were made of brass. When these feathers fell to earth, they would penetrate the skull of anyone unfortunate enough to be in the way. Then the birds would swoop down and devour their victim.

Hercules knew he didn't have enough arrows to kill all of them. That wasn't the only problem. Because the marsh was very unsteady, it was hard for him to get stable footing so he could fire his arrows at them. He found himself slipping ever deeper into the muck.

The goddess Athena (uh-THEE-nuh) saw Hercules' plight. She knew that Zeus liked Hercules and wanted to help him.

Giving him a brass rattle, she told him to climb to the top of a nearby hill and shake it. The noise panicked the birds, which quickly flew off. Hercules shot many of them with his arrows. The rest flew far away from Greece. They would never bother the Greeks again.

The seventh labor involved a huge white bull that lived on the island of Crete. The sea god Poseidon (poh-SIH-dun) had driven it mad. It rampaged around the countryside, threatening anyone who went outside. No one could tend the fields, and hardly any food grew.

Soon after arriving on Crete, as he was walking along a road, Hercules heard the bull charging him from behind. He jumped out of the way just in time. As the bull turned and charged again, Hercules jumped on its back. He grabbed the bull by the horns and

Hercules had to travel to the island of Crete to capture a bull that was terrorizing the inhabitants. It breathed fire and dug up crops while threatening to kill anyone it found in the open. As was the case with many of his other labors, Hercules had to bring back the animal alive.

wrestled it to the ground. Then he tied it up and tried to carry it onto a ship. For some reason, the bull didn't want to go aboard.

Hercules had an idea. He untied the bull, mounted it, and rode it into the sea. That was what it wanted. It swam all the way from Crete with Hercules on its back.

Eurystheus was afraid of the bull, and he was afraid that Poseidon would want vengeance if he sacrificed it. Instead he let it loose on the Plain of Marathon, where it went wild again. Finally Theseus (THEE-see-us), another great hero, managed to kill it.

Jason and the Golden Fleece

Jason's father Aeson (EE-son) was the rightful king of the land of Iolchus (ee-OL-kus), but Jason's cousin, Pelias (PEE-lee-us), had taken over the throne. Jason wanted to reclaim it for his father. Pelias told him that Aeson could have it back—after Jason went to the land of Colchis (KOL-kis) and secured the golden fleece of a ram that had been sacrificed.

Jason enlisted many of the greatest heroes of Greece—Hercules, Theseus, Orpheus (OR-fee-us), Castor, Polydeuces, and more—to come with him on the quest. Their ship was the *Argo*. Jason and his friends were known as the Argonauts.

Jason bringing Pelias
the golden fleece

The Argonauts had many adventures en route to Colchis. Hercules left the expedition at a relatively early stage. His servant, Hylas, was drawn into the depths of a freshwater spring by a water nymph. As the noted scholar Edith Hamilton explains, "Hercules sought him madly everywhere, shouting his name and plunging deeper and deeper into the forest away from the sea. . . . He did not come back, and finally the ship had to sail without him."[3]

When the Argonauts arrived at Colchis, the king, Aeëtes (eye-EE-teez), didn't want to give up the golden fleece. He gave Jason the chance to earn it by doing four tasks. He had to harness two very fierce bulls, then plow a field with them. He had to sow the furrows with dragon's teeth. The teeth would spring up and become an army—which he would have to destroy by himself.

Fortunately for Jason, the king's daughter Medea (mee-DEE-uh) fell in love with him. When the army attacked him, Medea gave him a stone. He threw it in the middle of the soldiers, and they killed each other. She also helped him cast a spell over the dragon that guarded the fleece.

As soon as he had the fleece, Jason headed home, taking Medea with him. His father had died, so the quest for the fleece had been in vain. Years later, after having two sons with Medea, Jason left her for another woman. Medea killed the sons and Jason's new love. Jason spent the rest of his life wandering aimlessly through Greece.

for your info

F.Y.I.

Picking the golden apples in the Garden of the Hesperides was one of
Hercules' most difficult labors. A deadly serpent named Ladon
(wrapped around the trunk) guarded the precious fruit. Hera was very
unhappy when Hercules killed Ladon. She transformed the serpent
into a constellation named Draco the Dragon, which is located close
to the Little Dipper.

HERCULES

CHAPTER 3

More Labor Days

Eurystheus was starting to get desperate. He couldn't believe that Hercules had survived for so long. He decided that since Hercules had sometimes had help, he would get some help himself. He turned to King Diomedes (dy-AH-meh-deez) of Thrace, who was an evil man. He had trained four mares to pull his chariot in war. When the battle was over, he would allow them to feed on the corpses of their enemies. Soon the mares refused to eat anything except human flesh, which created a problem in peacetime. Diomedes had a simple solution. He would have a banquet at his palace. When the guests fell asleep after eating and drinking, he would cut their throats and feed them to the mares.

Eurystheus told Hercules he had to capture the mares. Hercules asked some friends to come with him. Diomedes acted glad to see them, but Hercules knew he wasn't.

He and his friends hardly slept for fear that Diomedes would attack them while they were sleeping. They got up very early the next morning, crept into the stables, opened the doors, and drove the mares down to where their ship was beached. Diomedes and his men followed in hot pursuit, but Hercules cut a channel from the sea between him and his pursuers. The water rushed in, and Diomedes and his followers all drowned.

Meanwhile, Hercules had left Abderus (AB-duh-rus) alone with the mares. They had killed and eaten him. Outraged, Hercules grabbed Diomedes' body and fed it to the mares. He founded the city of Abdera (AB-duh-ruh) in honor of his friend. Then he tied the horses' muzzles shut and took them back to Eurystheus, who ordered them to be killed. He didn't want them to eat anyone in Mycenae.

The idea for the next labor came from Eurystheus' daughter Admete (ad-MEE-tee). She wanted the belt from the famous Amazon queen Hippolyte (hip-PAH-luh-tee) as a birthday present. Amazons were a race of fearsome female warriors. They were trained from birth in the arts of combat. According to legend, they all cut off their right breast so that it wouldn't get in the way when they drew their bow. The men did all the household chores: cooking, sewing, cleaning house, and so on. To make sure that the men didn't try to get away or challenge the women, their arms and legs were broken while they were still infants, which crippled them for life.

Eurystheus thought he had a win-win situation in this labor. If Hercules failed, he would finally be rid of him. If he succeeded, his daughter would have a nice birthday present.

At first, everything went well for Hercules. When he arrived in the land of the Amazons, he told Hippolyte why he wanted her belt. He was friendly and polite, and he stressed that his mission was peaceful. Hippolyte was impressed. She took off the belt and gave it to Hercules.

Hera didn't want things to go so smoothly. She disguised herself as one of the Amazons and spread a lie, saying that Hercules was really there to kidnap Hippolyte. The angry Amazons attacked Hercules and his men. During the battle, Hercules killed Hippolyte. He didn't understand why she had attacked him.

Hercules and his men managed to get back to their ship and sail away. But they weren't in a good mood. They didn't like all the killing they had just had to do to get a birthday present.

For the tenth labor, Eurystheus sent Hercules on a long voyage. He had to sail out of the Mediterranean to an island called Erythea (uh-REE-thee-uh, which means "the red")[1] off the western coast of modern-day Spain. There he would find the cattle of Geryon (GEE-ree-ohn). This fearsome monster had three huge heads and three big bodies on a single pair of legs. Hercules had to kill Geryon and bring back the cattle.

When Hercules tried to exit the Mediterranean at its western end, a series of cliffs blocked his way. He had to force them apart. To show what he had done, he left behind two rock pillars. To this day, they are known as the Pillars of Hercules. The waterway between them is the Strait of Gibraltar.[2]

To help Hercules, the sun god Helios let him borrow a golden goblet shaped like a water lily, which he sailed to the island.[3] Hercules killed the men guarding the herd. When Geryon appeared, Hercules took careful aim and fired his bow. The arrow pierced all three of Geryon's heads, and he fell, dead.

Now Hercules had to get the cattle home. It was long, difficult journey. He had many adventures involving those who tried to steal them, and at one point had to call on Zeus for help. Finally he got back to Mycenae. Eurystheus sacrificed all the cattle to honor the goddess Hera.

Eurystheus felt very confident about the eleventh labor. He was sure that he would finally be rid of Hercules. The task was to pick the Golden Apples of the Hesperides (hes-PEH-rih-dez). The Hesperides were the daughters of Atlas, an ancient giant who bore the heavens on his shoulders.

There were several challenges to the labor. The apple tree had been one of Hera's presents when she married Zeus, so Hercules would be stealing directly from the gods. That alone would put him in a great deal of trouble. Also, Ladon (LAY-don), a serpent or, according to some sources, a dragon with a hundred heads, guarded the tree. And no one even knew where the tree was.

Hercules spent many months wandering around the Mediterranean trying to find someone who could tell him where to look. Finally three nymphs called the Nereids (NEER-ee-idz) told him that their father, Nereus (NEER-ee-oos), the Old Man of the Sea, knew where the garden was.

Hercules grabbed him, but Nereus could shift shapes in an instant. First he became seawater, then a hot flame, and then a fierce

lion. Each time Hercules managed to hold on. Finally Nereus gave up. He returned to his original shape and told Hercules where the apple tree was. He told him to begin his quest by killing Ladon.

"Even then," Nereus cautioned, "you can't pick the apples yourself. You'll have to have the Hesperides do it for you. That way Hera can't seek revenge on you."

As he made his way to the land of the Hesperides, Hercules had many adventures. One of the most famous was with Antaeus (an-TEE-us), the son of Mother Earth and the sea god Poseidon. Because of his connection with the earth, Antaeus could never be defeated as long as he remained in contact with the earth. Hercules threw him to the ground a couple of times. Each time Antaeus got up stronger. Finally Hercules realized what he had to do. He lifted Antaeus off his feet. As Antaeus grew weaker, Hercules strangled him.

Eventually he found the garden where the tree was located. He killed Ladon, then went to find Atlas. Atlas agreed to ask his daughters to pick the apples, but he made Hercules hold the heavens on his shoulders while he was away.

Atlas soon returned with the precious fruit. Hercules wanted to give him the heavens back, but Atlas was glad to be rid of the weight. He was content to have Hercules keep holding it up. Atlas wasn't very smart, and Hercules thought he could trick him.

"Atlas, I need a better place to sit," he said. "Can you hold the heavens for just a moment while I shift positions? Also, I want to fold my lion's skin and put it on my shoulders. It will make the burden more comfortable."

"Sure," said the giant.

As soon as he was rid of the weight, Hercules grabbed the basket of fruit and took off.

Eurystheus was horrified that Hercules had returned. He knew if he kept the fruit, Hera would be very angry with him. He ordered Hercules to take the fruit back to the Hesperides.

Now it was time for the final labor. Desperate, Eurystheus told Hercules to go to the Underworld, the dark and gloomy kingdom deep inside the earth where all dead people were consigned. Once he was there, he was to kidnap Cerberus (SIR-bur-us), the three-headed dog who guarded the door. Cerberus made sure that no one could escape once they had entered.

To even get to Cerberus, Hercules had to get past Hades (HAY-deez), ruler of the Underworld. Hercules shot Hades with an arrow. As the famous Greek poet Homer explains, Hades was "stabbed with agony, grief-stricken to the heart, the shaft driven into his massive shoulder."[4] He agreed to let Hercules take Cerberus. But, he said,

For his final labor, Hercules had to seize the three-headed dog named Cerberus. Cerberus allowed the spirits of the dead to enter the Underworld but kept them from leaving. Even though the dog was very vicious, Hercules had to capture it with his bare hands.

Hercules wore the head and skin of the Nemean Lion on many of his labors. It made him even stronger than he was normally.

Hercules had to use his bare hands to capture the horrible hound. No weapons would be allowed.

Cerberus slobbered as he watched Hercules approach. Suddenly he pounced. But Hercules was ready. He threw his lion's skin—which he always wore—over Cerberus' three heads. That subdued the dog. Then he carried it back to Mycenae.

The sight of the dog was too much for Eurystheus. He ran away. As he fled, he shouted over his shoulder, "Get rid of that thing! Send him back where he came from! Right now!"

Hades

Hades was the lord of the Underworld. Sometimes the Underworld was also called Hades. His queen, Persephone, was only a part-time monarch. She dwelled in the world for six months every year, bringing the seasons of spring and summer. When she went back to Hades, autumn and winter reflected her absence.

Hades

When people died and were ready to enter the Underworld, they had to cross the river Styx (STIKS). The boatman Charon (KAYR-on) would ferry them across—if they could pay for their passage. The price was an obol, a small Greek coin. Friends and relatives of the deceased person were careful to place an obol under the lifeless tongue for the funeral. People who had no friends or relatives were stuck—literally. They couldn't make the crossing to the Underworld, nor could they return to the world of the living.

Cerberus, the three-headed dog, waited on the other side of the river, guarding the entrance to Hades' palace. Just before entering the palace, the dead person also faced three judges: Minos, Rhadamanthys, and Aeacus.

Hades was not really a place that anyone really wanted to be. It was gloomy and sunless. The famous Greek hero Achilles—who was killed during the Trojan War—once told a visitor:

> By god, I'd rather slave on earth for another man—
>   some dirt-poor tenant farmer who scrapes to keep alive—
>   than rule down here over all the breathless dead.[5]

Many people were afraid to even mention the name of Hades. They thought it could bring bad luck. Instead they called him Pluton, which means "wealthy." The name came from the fact that precious metals such as gold and silver existed under the earth, and Hades had control of them. The Romans called him Pluto.

Hercules put on a robe that had been treated with a deadly poison. He felt as if his body were on fire. He tried to rip off the robe, but his efforts worsened the pain. His suffering could only end with the death of his mortal part.

HERCULES

CHAPTER 4

Further Adventures and Finale

At last Hercules was free, but it didn't take him long to get into trouble again.

He went to an island called Euboea (yoo-BEE-uh). He had heard that the king there, Eurytus (YUR-ih-tus), would give his daughter Iole (EYE-oh-lee) to anyone who could outshoot him with a bow and arrow. Hercules easily won the challenge, but Eurytus refused to allow the marriage to take place. He knew what had happened to Hercules' first wife and children.

Hercules angrily left Euboea. Not long afterward, Eurytus realized that some of his horses were missing. He thought that Hercules had stolen them. His son Iphitus (IH-fih-tus), who had wanted Hercules to marry Iole, volunteered to go see Hercules and try to clear up the situation. Hercules went with Iphitus to the top of a high tower, then pushed him over the edge. Iphitus died when he hit the ground.

Once again, Hercules had killed an innocent person. Once again, Hercules visited the Oracle at Delphi. Once again, he learned that he had to serve someone. This time there would be no dangerous labors. He was taken as a common slave and sold to the highest bidder.

The highest bidder turned out to be Queen Omphale (OM-fah-lee), of Lydia in Africa. She was content to let him work. She did ask him to rid her kingdom of robbers, which was very easy for him to do. At the end of three years, Omphale let Hercules go.

He had a series of adventures, including one at Troy. His exploits left Priam as king—Priam would remain the ruler throughout the Trojan War. He also sought vengeance against the people who had

According to some versions of the Hercules legend, Queen Omphale took him as her lover. She also made him wear women's clothes and do women's work, such as spinning. The cherub in the lower left corner holds up a spindle with yarn to Hercules.

wronged him during the previous years, including Augeas, who had refused to pay him for cleaning his stables.

Then Hercules married Deianeira (dee-yuh-NYE-ruh). One day he set off on a journey with her. They came to a deep river. Hercules could swim across the river, but Deianeira couldn't. Nessus, a centaur, offered to help them.

"Let me take Deianeira on my back," said Nessus.

When Nessus got to the other side, he tried to run off with her. Hercules drew his bow and shot him through the heart. As he lay dying, he whispered to Deianeira to take some of his blood. He said it would serve as a charm to keep Hercules in love with her.

Hercules still wasn't through with Eurytus. He attacked the city, killed the king, and took Iole as a prisoner. To honor his victory, he wanted to sacrifice some bulls. He needed to wear a special robe during the ceremony, which Deianeira had. Hercules sent a messenger to her to fetch the robe.

Deianeira was very jealous of Iole. She knew that Hercules had wanted to marry the other woman. To keep him faithful, Deianeira smeared the robe with the centaur's blood.

Nessus had lied. His blood was not a charm but a deadly poison. In his play *The Trachiniae* (*The Women of Trachis*), the Greek playwright Sophocles describes what happened when Hercules put on the robe and began the ceremony:

> His whole body began to sweat,
> [the] shirt, as tight as any builder's mortise [a securely fastened
>   builder's joint]
> clung to his ribs, and then to every limb.
> On every bone came cramping, torturing fire,
> as the serpentine and deadly venom gnawed.
> He screamed in pain . . .
> Yet not a soul dared to approach the hero,
> now squirming in anguish, groveling on the earth,
> now starting up in sharp spasmodic pain.
> The cries of Heracles reechoed from the rocks
> on every side.[1]

He couldn't rip it off. Nothing helped, not even leaping into a river. He knew he was dying.

His son Hyllus (HYE-lus) carried him to the top of a mountain and built a funeral pyre. Hercules lay down on top of it.

Zeus was watching from Mount Olympus, the home of the gods. He decided that only Hercules' mother's part would die, and the rest would become immortal. This process of becoming a god is called

Mount Olympus was believed to be the home of the Greek gods and goddesses. Located in northern Greece, it is more than 9,000 feet high. Many people climb it every year.

apotheosis (uh-pah-thee-OH-sis). Zeus sent down a chariot to bring Hercules to Mount Olympus. Even Hera was finally ready to receive him. She gave him her daughter Hebe (HEE-bee), the goddess of youth, in marriage. Zeus made the Hercules constellation in his honor.

As poet Robert Graves describes, Hercules had one primary job on Mount Olympus: He was the porter of heaven. He "never tires of standing at the Olympian gates, towards nightfall, waiting for Artemis' return from the chase. He greets her merrily, and hauls the heaps of prey out of her chariot, frowning and wagging a finger in disapproval if he finds only harmless goats and hares. 'Shoot wild boars,' he says, 'that trample down crops and gash orchard-trees; shoot man-killing bulls, and lions and wolves. But what harm have goats and hares done us?'"[2]

Sophocles

The famous Greek playwright Sophocles was probably born about 496 BCE. It's likely that his father was well-to-do, possibly a merchant who was wealthy enough to afford a large house just outside of Athens. Sophocles was very well educated, and he also reportedly became a good wrestler.

Sophocles

He led a choir of boys to celebrate the Greek victory over the Persians at the Battle of Salamis (SAH-luh-mis) in 480. Twelve years later he began entering the Dionysia (dy-oh-NY-zhyuh), Athens' annual dramatic competition. He won first place that year, and repeated that honor nearly twenty times during the course of his career. Scholars believe that he wrote about 120 plays during that time. Only seven survive.

He had a reputation as a good actor and appeared on stage in many of his plays. He was responsible for several innovations. Before his time, there were only two actors and a chorus on stage at any one time. Sophocles added a third actor.

He also changed the form of drama. Ancient Greek playwrights wrote trilogies—three plays about a single theme. Sophocles introduced the idea of a single play about a single theme. It soon became the way in which most plays were presented.

His most famous play is *Oedipus* (EH-duh-pus) *Rex*, or *Oedipus the King*. It is part of a trilogy, which also includes *Oedipus at Colonus* and *Antigone*. In *Oedipus Rex*, Oedipus' parents—King Laius (LAY-us) and Queen Jocasta (joh-KAS-tuh)—are warned before his birth that he will grow up to kill his father and marry his mother. They abandon him on a mountain when he is born. He survives and grows up to fulfill the prophecy, although he doesn't realize what he has done. Nor does Jocasta. When they do realize what has happened, Jocasta hangs herself and Oedipus blinds himself. For the rest of his life he wanders the countryside as a beggar.

Sophocles held some important civic positions. He was treasurer of Athens. He spent a year as one of the city's generals. He even served as a priest for Asclepius (uh-SKLEE-pee-us), the god of medicine and healing.[3] He died about the year 405 BCE.

While seeking the Golden Apples of the Hesperides, Hercules had to hold up the heavens for a brief period. He used the Nemean Lion's skin to help cushion the burden.

HERCULES

CHAPTER 5

The Impact of Hercules

The story of Hercules probably began as a local legend about an especially strong man. As the story was told and retold over the centuries, his exploits began to grow and expand, until he became a famous hero.

It's likely that in this respect the stories are similar to stories about Paul Bunyan. Many people believe that Paul Bunyan was a real-life logger. He lived in Canada and the upper Midwest in the mid-nineteenth century. Loggers would tell stories about this man around campfires after a hard day's work in the woods. Each time, the hero would take on larger-than-life qualities. Finally Paul Bunyan was a tall-tale hero.

Many scholars believe that the Hercules stories began during the Greek Dark Ages, approximately 1200 to 800 BCE. It was a dangerous time. People didn't have much protection against their enemies. They would have wanted to rely on someone much stronger than themselves to make their daily lives safer.

But Hercules was more than just a man with lots of muscles. "The mythical [Hercules] was the one true [Greek] hero," notes classics professor G. Karl Galinsky. "As a mythological hero, [Hercules] replaced, in many towns, local heroes whose exploits promptly were absorbed into his mythological baggage train. Because he was the national hero of Greece, all kinds of characteristics were attributed or transferred to him."[1]

Because of his status as a "national hero," there are several important elements in the story of Hercules. Professor W. B. Stanford explains one of them: "We are exploring the ideals, hopes and fears

of a man faced with the arduous task of protecting and preserving human society from its natural enemies."[2]

Professor Barry B. Powell notes, "As the best-loved of all Greek heroes, [Hercules] was summoned as a god to turn away disease, human and animal attack, and every kind of harm. . . . He is the tough guy, the strongest man on earth . . . the animal-slayer who made the world safe by destroying dangerous beasts."[3]

Many of his feats were literally death defying, so there is another significance as well. It is natural for people to be afraid of dying. Hercules faced death many times and always managed to survive. That would have been very inspirational to people who listened to his story. It would have given them hope that they too could put off their own death for as long as possible—and possibly become immortal.

The Hercules story is much more than a description of dangerous and serious life events. The Greeks enjoyed laughing, and there are many comic aspects to the Hercules myth.

One aspect is the panic-stricken reaction of Eurystheus nearly every time that Hercules comes back with one of his "trophies." The king either hides in his bronze jar or orders Hercules to get away from him. He certainly doesn't act very kingly.

Another humorous element occurs in one of the versions of Hercules' childhood. Supposedly as a baby he was taken in secret to see Hera. Not knowing who he was, she allowed him to suckle at her breast. Hercules chomped down with his very powerful jaws. Hera howled in pain. Much of her milk spilled out into the heavens, where it became the Milky Way.

A third involves Omphale. Even though he was her slave, she also had a love affair with him. Sometimes they liked to dress up in each other's clothes. One night a god named Pan snuck into the house where they were staying. It was too dark to see anything. Pan felt a woman's garment and thought it belonged to Omphale. He was wrong. Hercules was wearing it. Hercules got very angry when Pan tried to get in bed with him. He kicked him against the far wall

The labors of Hercules were a popular subject for artists who decorated Greek vases. Many of these artists liked to show humorous episodes, such as Eurystheus jumping into a jar because he was afraid of Cerberus.

of the room. The thought of their mighty hero wearing women's clothing and being mistaken for a woman would have been hilarious to the Greeks as they listened to the story.

His story goes back many centuries. He is mentioned in the *Iliad* of Homer, which was recorded around 800 BCE. The heroic Achilles says:

> For my own death, I'll meet it freely—whenever Zeus
> and the other deathless gods would like to bring it on!
> Not even [Hercules] fled his death, for all his power,
> favorite son as he was to Father Zeus the King.
> Fate crushed him and Hera's savage anger.[4]

His apotheosis seems to have been added to the myth after Homer recorded the *Iliad*. It's also likely that the number of labors—as well as Hercules' other exploits—grew over the centuries. The earliest indication that there were twelve labors is the temple of Zeus in Olympia (the site of the Olympic Games), which was built in about 470 BCE. A stone panel called a metope (MEH-tuh-pee) was located above each of the twelve pillars. Each metope had an illustration of one of the twelve labors.

After that, both the number of labors and the order in which they occurred became fairly standardized. There is a certain logic in their progression. The first six take place relatively close to Mycenae. The seventh (the Cretan Bull) goes more than one hundred miles to the south. The next three go hundreds of miles north, east, and west, respectively. The final two are in heaven (the Apples of the Hesperides) and hell (capturing Cerberus).

Many if not most of the stories tell about things that never happened, although the ancient Greeks may have believed they took place in their distant history. One of the purposes of the myths was to entertain people. Just as people today flock to theaters to see horror films, Greek audiences liked to see things that they themselves would never consider doing or would be afraid to witness in real life.

The Greeks also liked references to contemporary events. For example, in 416 BCE, the city of Athens savagely attacked the inhabitants of the island of Milos. All the male adults on Milos were killed; the women and children were enslaved. Many citizens of Athens didn't approve of the slaughter. They thought it was a monstrous crime against humanity.

Many scholars believe that the great Athenian playwright Euripides wrote his play *Madness of Heracles* to reflect the horror that these Athenians felt. The Milesians had done almost nothing to deserve their fate. They were basically helpless in the face of the Athenians' superior strength. To Euripides, it closely approximated what Hercules had done to his wife Megara and their children. For example, Euripides describes how Hercules (Heracles) kills his second child:

> An arrow Heracles aimed at the second, crouched by the altar,
>   hoping, in vain, to hide there unobserved.
> Before the arrow could fly, the poor boy reached for a hug,
> but fell, and vainly tried to clutch at his father's knees.
> "Oh dearest Daddy," he cried, "Daddy, please don't hit
>   me! . . . I'm your own little boy!"
> Heracles only rolled his wide and Gorgon eyes.
> The child was too close as a mark for his deadly bow;
> like a blacksmith at his anvil, Heracles whirled his club
> down on the boy's fair hair and shattered the bones
>   beneath.[5]

To Euripides and many of his fellow Athenians, their city had acted just as madly as Hercules had—and it was inexcusable. Athens had used its superior strength to kill people who were as defenseless as Hercules' son had been.

Many other writers and artists have used him to help make their points. Several of Shakespeare's plays mention Hercules or use themes that first appear in the many stories about him.

Some versions of his story show him sleeping during his travels for the labors. An army of Pygmies (a race of exceptionally small people) tries to attack him while he is sleeping. They tie ropes around his body. When Hercules wakes up, he easily snaps the bindings.[6] Jonathan Swift uses this same idea in his book *Gulliver's Travels*. Tiny people called Lilliputians do pretty much the same thing to the hero, Lemuel Gulliver. Since he isn't anywhere near as strong as Hercules, the bindings are effective. He becomes helpless and can't move.

George Frideric Handel, whose eighteenth-century masterpiece *Messiah* is performed all over the world at Christmastime, wrote an

oratorio called *Hercules*. Twentieth-century poets T.S. Eliot, Archibald MacLeish, and Ezra Pound have featured Hercules in their works. Also, as Galinsky points out, "This kind of hero, exalted in his physical power, defeated by a woman, and headed for self-extinction is a known figure on the twentieth-century American stage, especially from the plays of Eugene O'Neill."[7]

His influence can be seen outside literature and music as well. In the late fourth century BCE, Greek leader Alexander the Great began conquering much of the known world. He issued coins that showed him wearing the pelt of the Nemean Lion. The coins conveyed a not too subtle message to Alexander's enemies: Just as Hercules overcame every obstacle in his path, these enemies didn't have much of a chance against Alexander and his army.

Hercules is the subject of numerous young people's books, movies, TV series, and much more. A number of words and phrases today reflect how well known he is. A herculean task is one that seems almost impossible. A person with herculean strength is much stronger than the average person. An Augean stable is an especially messy situation.

Hercules shows what happens when a person or a country becomes especially strong. This strength can be used for evil purposes. The Greeks hoped that if people realized this, they would use their individual and social strength for good purposes. Instead of destroying things, they would want to build and create things. That way everyone would benefit.

A Brief Greek History

Greek history as we know it begins nearly 4,000 years ago. People from the north who had been displaced from their homes settled there, and within 500 years had taken over much of modern-day Greece. During this era, called the Bronze Age, weapons and other valuable objects were being made of bronze (a compound of copper and tin).

For several hundred years, the main feature of each Greek settlement was a large palace surrounded by very thick walls built of immense stones. The palace was usually at the highest point of the area inside the walls. It was centered on a large throne room. The kings and other important families enjoyed a great degree of comfort. Most people lived outside the walls, often on small farms. In times of danger they would come inside the walls.

For reasons that scholars still don't know, around the twelfth century BCE, something happened to change this civilization. People began to live in small settlements, where there was very little luxury or culture. They were just barely able to scrape by. This period is known as the Dark Ages of Greece.

When the Dark Ages ended, people began living in larger settlements called poleis (POH-lays). Most scholars believe this is when Homer wrote down his famous works, the *Iliad* and the *Odyssey*. These poems depict an earlier, heroic time. It's likely that Homer wanted to remind his readers and listeners how important Greece could be.

Over the next few centuries the Greeks began building up an important civilization. The poleis became larger, more numerous, and much more prosperous.

The Parthenon (top) in Athens, Greece

After defeating the invading Persians early in the fifth century BCE, the Greeks—especially in Athens—entered what became known as the Golden Age. It was marked by democracy, art, and literature. Many famous buildings such as the Parthenon in Athens were built during this era.

The Greeks often fought among themselves. Finally a full-scale war, the Peloponnesian (pel-uh-puh-NEE-zhyun) War, began in 431 BCE. The Spartans and their allies defeated the Athenians twenty-seven years later. Greece never regained its former splendor.

Chapter 1. The Legend Begins

1. Robert Graves, *The Greek Myths* (New York: Penguin Books, 1992), p. 241.

2. Michael Grant and John Hazel, *Who's Who in Classical Mythology* (New York: Routledge, 2002), p. 22.

3. Ibid., pp. 130-131.

4. Ibid., p. 148.

Chapter 2. Labor Days

1. Hercules' Second Labor: The Lernaean Hydra, http://www.perseus.tufts.edu/Herakles/hydra.html

2. Michael Grant and John Hazel, *Who's Who in Classical Mythology* (New York: Routledge, 2002), p. 164.

3. Edith Hamilton, *Mythology* (New York: Warner Books, 1999), p. 125.

Chapter 3. More Labor Days

1. Michael Grant and John Hazel, *Who's Who in Classical Mythology* (New York: Routledge, 2002), p. 143.

2. Hercules' Tenth Labor: The Cattle of Geryon, http://www.perseus.tufts.edu/Herakles/cattle.html

3. Robert Graves, *The Greek Myths* (New York: Penguin Books, 1992), p. 495.

4. Homer, *The Iliad*, translated by Robert Fagles (New York: Penguin Books, 1990), p. 177.

5. Homer, *The Odyssey*, translated by Robert Fagles (New York: Penguin Books, 1996), p. 265.

Chapter 4. Further Adventures and Finale

1. Barry P. Powell, *Classical Myth* (Upper Saddle River, New Jersey: Pearson Educational, 2004), pp. 382–383.

2. Robert Graves, *The Greek Myths* (New York: Penguin Books, 1992), p. 565.

3. Helen Shaw, "Sophocles: A Mythic Life," http://www.amrep.org/past/antigone/antigone3.html

Chapter 5. The Impact of Hercules

1. G. Karl Galinsky, *The Herakles Theme: The Adaptations of the Hero in Literature from Homer to the Twentieth Century* (Totowa, New Jersey: Rowman and Littlefield, 1972), p. 3.

2. Ibid., p. x.

3. Barry P. Powell, *Classical Myth* (Upper Saddle River, New Jersey: Pearson Educational, 2004), p. 386.

4. Homer, *The Iliad*, translated by Robert Fagles (New York: Penguin Books, 1990), p. 471.

5. Powell, p. 362.

6. Thomas Cahill, *Sailing the Wine-Dark Sea: Why the Greeks Matter* (New York: Doubleday, 2003), p. 29.

7. Galinsky, p. 243.

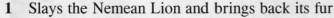

TWELVE LABORS OF HERCULES

1 Slays the Nemean Lion and brings back its fur
2 Slays the Lernaean Hydra
3 Captures the Ceryneian Hind
4 Captures the Erymanthian Boar
5 Cleans the Augean stables in a single day
6 Slays the Stymphalian Birds
7 Captures the Cretan Bull
8 Steals the Mares of Diomedes
9 Obtains the Girdle of Hippolyte
10 Obtains the Cattle of Geryon
11 Steals the Golden Apples of the Hesperides
12 Captures Cerberus, the guardian dog of Hades

FURTHER READING

For Young Adults

Balzer, Elizabeth. *Hercules: Illustrated Classic*. New York: Disney Press, 1997.

McCaughrean, Geraldine. *Hercules*. Chicago: Cricket Books, 2005.

Moroz, Georges. *Hercules: The Twelve Labors*. New York: Yearling Press, 1998.

Riordan, James. *The Twelve Labors of Hercules*. Brookfield, Connecticut: The Millbrook Press, 1997.

Weisbrot, Rob. *Hercules: The Legendary Journeys*. New York: Doubleday Books for Young Readers, 1998.

Whiting, Jim. *Jason*. Profiles in Greek and Roman Mythology. Hockessin, Delaware: Mitchell Lane Publishers, 2007.

Works Consulted

Cahill, Thomas. *Sailing the Wine-Dark Sea: Why the Greeks Matter*. New York: Doubleday, 2003.

Edmunds, Lowell (editor). *Approaches to Greek Myth*. Baltimore, Maryland: The Johns Hopkins University Press, 1990.

Galinsky, G. Karl. *The Herakles Theme: The Adaptations of the Hero in Literature from Homer to the Twentieth Century*. Totowa, New Jersey: Rowman and Littlefield, 1972.

Grant, Michael, and John Hazel. *Who's Who in Classical Mythology*. New York: Routledge, 2002.

Graves, Robert. *The Greek Myths*. New York: Penguin Books, 1992.

Hamilton, Edith. *Mythology*. New York: Warner Books, 1999.

Homer. *The Iliad*. Translated by Robert Fagles. New York: Penguin Books, 1990.

———. *The Odyssey*. Translated by Robert Fagles. New York: Penguin Books, 1996.

Kerényi, C. *Heroes of the Greeks*. Translated by Professor H. J. Rose. London: Thames and Hudson, 1959.

Lefkowitz, Mary. *Greek Gods, Human Lives: What We Can Learn from Myths*. New Haven, Connecticut: Yale University Press, 2003.

Powell, Barry P. *Classical Myth*. Upper Saddle River, New Jersey: Pearson Educational, 2004.

On the Internet

Greek Mythology: The Labors of Hercules
http://www.mythweb.com/hercules/index.html

Hercules in Painting
http://www.temple.edu/classics/herpaint.html

Hercules: Greece's Greatest Hero
http://www.perseus.tufts.edu/Herakles/

Jason, the Argonauts and the Golden Fleece
http://www.mythweb.com/heroes/jason/index.html

Livius Picture Archive-Labors of Hercules
http://www.livius.org/a/heracles/heracles1.html

Porter, John. "The Iliad and the Greek Bronze Age."
http://homepage.usask.ca/~jrp638/CourseNotes/HomBA.html

Shaw, Helen. "Sophocles: A Mythic Life."
http://www.amrep.org/past/antigone/antigone3.html

Timeless Myths—Heracles
http://www.timelessmyths.com/classical/heracles.html

anvil (AN-vul)—An iron block on which metal is shaped.

apotheosis (uh-pah-thee-OH-sis)—In mythology, the process by which a mortal becomes a god.

cauterize (CAW-tur-ize)—To destroy tissue by the quick application of intense heat.

fleece—A coat of wool that covers the skin of an animal such as a sheep.

funeral pyre (FYOON-rul PYR)—A gathering of wood on which a dead body is burned in a funeral ceremony.

Gorgon (GOR-gun)—A mythical creature with snakes for hair; looking at one turns people to stone.

lyre (LY-ur)—A handheld stringed instrument, similar to a small harp.

oracle (OR-uh-kul)—A person through which hidden meanings or concealed knowledge is revealed; also, the shrine in which such a person may be consulted.

oratorio (or-uh-TOR-ee-oh)—A long musical work for chorus and soloists without any scenery or action on stage.

serpentine (SER-pen-teen)—From or like a snake (serpent).

sow (SOH)—To plant.

Zodiac (ZOH-dee-ak)—The band of twelve constellations through which the sun seems to travel during the year.